Take a trip to SPAIN

Jonathan Rutland

General Editor
Henry Pluckrose

Franklin Watts
London New York Sydney Toronto

Words about Spain

Alhambra Palace

Barcelona
bull-fighting

Calle de Alcalá
castanets
cave homes
centimos
Christopher
   Columbus

dates

fiesta
figs
flamenco dancing

Granada

Holy Week
   Festival

lace-making

Madrid
maize
matadors
Moors

olives
oranges

paella

Pamplona
peseta
Plaza de
   Cataluña

Ramblas

Segovia
Seville
sherry
sugar cane

'Talgo'
Tarifa
Toledo

Franklin Watts Limited
12a Golden Square
London W1

SBN UK edition: 85166 861 5
SBN US edition: 531 00991 2
Library of Congress Catalog Card No:
80 52718

Copyright © 1980 Franklin Watts Limited
Reprinted 1983

The publisher would like to thank the
following for kind permission to reproduce
photographs: J. Allan Cash: Barnaby's
Picture Library; Jonathan Rutland;
Spanish National Tourist Office; Zefa.

Maps by Brian and Constance Dear.

Printed in England by E T Heron & Co Ltd,
Silver End, Witham, Essex

Every year millions of people visit
Spain. Some people like to lie on the
sandy beaches. Others explore the
many interesting towns and cities.
Visitors to Barcelona can ride in a
carriage drawn by a horse.

Madrid is the capital of Spain. The Calle de Alcalá is one of the main streets. In the early morning it is busy with traffic. In Spain some people begin work at eight o'clock.

4

The Royal Palace is in the middle
of Madrid, but the King and his
family do not live there. For many
years there was no King. He
returned to Spain in 1975.

This picture shows some Spanish
stamps and money. There are
100 centimos in a peseta.

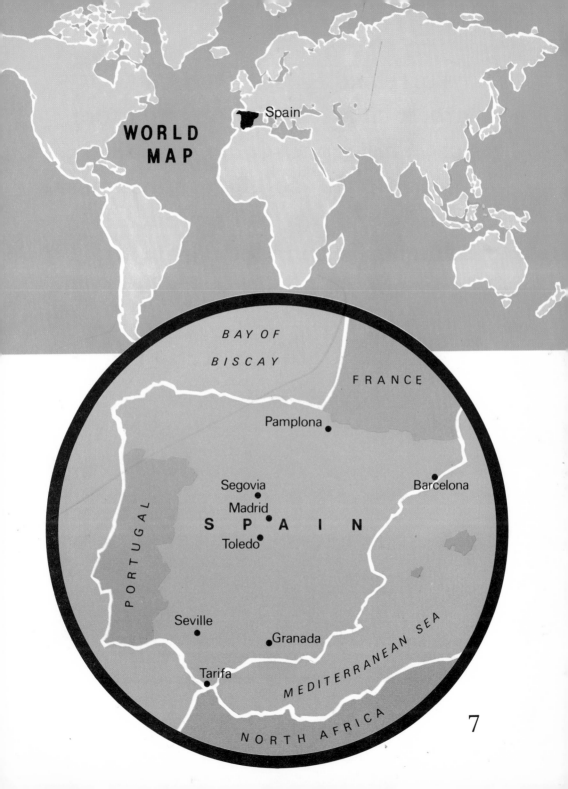

WORLD
MAP

Spain

BAY OF

BISCAY

FRANCE

Pamplona

Segovia

Barcelona

Madrid

S P A I N

PORTUGAL

Toledo

Seville

Granada

Tarifa

MEDITERRANEAN SEA

NORTH AFRICA

7

Barcelona is Spain's second largest city. It is also an important port. Christopher Columbus sailed to America in the 1400s in a Spanish ship. People can visit a replica of Columbus' ship in the port in Barcelona.

The Plaza de Cataluña, in the Ramblas, is Barcelona's main square. As it is so busy there is often a policeman to direct the traffic. In the Ramblas there are many open-air stalls.

Spain has many towns with
narrow streets and old buildings.
Toledo is an ancient town near
Madrid.

Seville is an old town in the south. The palm trees are a sign of the hot climate. Oranges are grown in the region and Seville oranges are often used to make marmalade.

Many towns, like Segovia, have stone walls around them. Often there is a castle inside the walls. Segovia's castle was built 500 years ago. Segovia's aquaduct is even older. It was built by the Ancient Romans.

About 500 years ago part of
Spain was ruled by the Moors. The
Moors came from Africa. They built
many beautiful buildings, like the
Alhambra Palace at Granada.

Paella is a dish made from rice mixed with tomatoes, peppers and peas. Sometimes meat or fish is added. Spanish people eat their main meal late in the evening. Beforehand, people meet at outdoor cafés for a chat.

Spanish children begin school
when they are six. Many young
children wear smocks to keep their
clothes clean.

Most houses have balconies where people can sit outside. The windows have blinds or shutters to keep the houses cool.

Many Spanish homes are painted white to reflect the heat of the sun.

The winters in northern Spain may be very cold, so some people put windows around the balcony. The windows are closed in the winter.

Some people in Spain are very poor. They live much as their ancestors did hundreds of years ago. People living in the poorer towns and villages often do their washing in a nearby stream.

In the hot south, some people live
in cave homes cut out of the rock.
Cave homes are very cool inside.

Bull-fighting is a popular sport. Before the fight begins, the matadors parade in the bull ring. The matadors use red capes to make the bull angry. Then they use long spears to weaken the bull before they kill it.

During the Bull Festival in Pamplona, the bulls are driven through the streets and around the bull ring. People try to keep out of the reach of the bull.

Each district has its traditional costume. Long ago it was worn in daily life. Today it is kept for special occasions like fiestas. Fiestas are a mixture of fair and carnival.

Many fiestas are religious festivals. During Holy Week in Seville people walk through the streets dressed in long cloaks and tall pointed hats.

Dancing is very popular and an occasion for wearing traditional costume. Each region has its own dances and many towns have dancing teams. In flamenco dancing the dancers stamp their feet and play castanets.

Although the summers are very
hot, snow falls on the mountains
in winter.

Many people like to go ski-ing.
The ski lift takes the skiers to the
top of the mountains.

There are many ports along the Spanish coastline. These ports are full of fishing boats. From Tarifa in the south, Africa can be seen in the distance.

There are also many fine beaches
on Spain's coast. The holiday
resorts are crowded with tourists
during the long, hot, summer. There
are many large hotels and
swimming pools.

Madrid is at the middle of the
network of main roads and railways.
Spain's most famous high-speed
luxury train is the 'Talgo'.

Farming people have little money and many use horses, not tractors, in the fields. Some farmers use donkeys to take their produce to towns. Town people also often use donkeys to carry their goods.

Farmers in Spain grow many
kinds of fruit and vegetables.
Maize is grown in central Spain.
After the maize has been picked it is
left to dry in the sun.

There are many vineyards in Spain. The grapes are made into wine and sherry. In the south farmers grow cotton, oranges, sugar cane, dates and olives. Figs are also left to dry in the sun, like the maize.

Index